WING CHUN MADE EASY

Richard Wonnacott

Published by New Generation Publishing in 2020

Copyright © Richard Wonnacott 2020

First Edition

The author asserts the moral right under the Copyright, Designs and Patents Act 1988 to be identified as the author of this work.

All Rights reserved. No part of this publication may be reproduced, stored in a retrieval system or transmitted, in any form or by any means without the prior consent of the author, nor be otherwise circulated in any form of binding or cover other than that which it is published and without a similar condition being imposed on the subsequent purchaser.

ISBN 978-1-80031-588-4

www.newgeneration-publishing.com

WHY WING CHUN MADE EASY.

Firstly, this isn't a book about me or my achievements. It's not a book with unnecessary pages of drivel. Its contents match the training, BASIC. It's about Wing Chun, not just how simple or basic it is. But how devastating it can be. Wing Chun honesty if you like.

I have been lucky enough to train with many great Sifus of different lineages. Many world renowned, many not so. Whether it be for long periods of time, just the odd few weeks here and there or on seminars both here in the UK and overseas. All this done alongside attending my usual classes of course.

What I've seen and learned over the years, is that alongside the good of Wing Chun, there is the not so good, in some cases very poor, and there is a lot of that. Unfortunately, it's the poor Wing Chun that is getting the publicity. Making it laughable to some, questioning its effectiveness.

It's because of this, and with lots of frustration from my own personal training, that I felt it needed addressing. Like most of us I'm sure.

I've erased a lot of the stuff I was shown and taught, seen or demonstrated, that I think is pointless so I have removed it from my training. All the fancy pointless stuff that has been added over the years to sell Wing Chun and make it look good has gone.

I personally think it's down to a few reasons:

People adding stuff from other styles, systems, to drag out the learning of Wing Chun, or worse still, the so called Sifu not learning it fully themselves then adding what they THINK it is. Or the ones just wanting that SIFU status. Not learnt it fully but wanting to be SIFU. As if that makes a difference.

Or, the 3rd reason, financial. The more levels, grades, belts, the longer it takes to complete, the more money spent. Which straight away detracts from Wing Chun's most important rule – it's very basic.

Everybody claims Wing Chun to be a basic, straightforward, devastating art but some of those same people are making it flowery, attractive and adding all sorts to it.

It's what is making this system look bad, and worse, act bad. Making it insufficient.

Over a very long period of time I have gone from student to teacher, I've gone over and over what works, what doesn't work. Seeing the guys I'm teaching and training alongside doing things that I was made to do, realising it to be a pointless waste of time. And on top of that, frustrated with class structure too. Poor all round.

I was carrying out the worst of the worst, that dreaded saying it seems many foolishly abide by:

WE DO IT THIS WAY BECAUSE IT'S ALWAYS BEEN DONE THIS WAY.

Well I choose to not go along with this saying any more, no longer following the crowd.

So with all this in mind, I decided to make a student programme with class structure, no unnecessary rubbish, or flowery crap as they say, taking away lots of things I knew was not needed. There was loads that needed to go.

Lots I had taught previously. GONE.

I wanted a Wing Chun that works, a COMPLETE WING CHUN if you like. So I sat down and, over a very long period of time, put pen to paper.

Thus we are here, a programme that is very basic, no frills, no add-ons. If it's in my levels here, then it's needed, if it's not then it's not needed. Everything is used, be it in a straight out toe-to-toe fight or in a self-defence situation. It's put to the test. And works.

I have put this into practice with myself and also my students. It's very understandable and straightforward. Adaptable for children too.

Class and students have structure. I struggled for long enough trying to get a great class regime which both myself and students could embrace and find easy to follow. These levels do that. Helping to bring on a student not only QUICKLY but with QUALITY. Which is what Wing Chun is supposed to be.

Show some dedication. Try it out, see how it goes. It will improve you. Even if it just helps you to master the basics of Wing Chun.

FEAR NOT THE MAN WHO PRACTISES 10,000 KICKS, FEAR THE MAN WHO TRAINS RICHARD WONNACOTT WING CHUN.

BEFORE WE BEGIN:

Some things to go over before we start going through the training. Firstly, you can warm up how ever you wish, it's advisable that you do. We all have our own thoughts on warming up. Make it your own, your preference. Some like to use tai chi, some like to go all out with press-ups, burpees and so forth. Whichever you prefer.

Remember, there is a difference between being fit and being fighting fit, having boxed myself I know the difference. What I train for now is that I can at least be able to defend myself without blowing through my ears.

My personal training now consists of some weight training to keep my muscle tone, just enough to stop muscle atrophy, as what happens with age. My Wing Chun forms keep my tendons and ligaments in shape and I practise yoga, to keep me subtle. I find the three complement each other very well. That's my fitness routine at this stage of my life.

There is no section on fitness, my aim here is Wing Chun basics only. I'm not going to cover bag or pad work in this book, nor any other training. Obviously I have warm-up and cool-down exercises, conditioning drills, fight-ready exercises for classes. This most definitely needs to be part of a class.

So it's up to you to get all this done, as well as following the levels themselves. Now some points on the levels we are going to train along to:

Firstly, it is not a case of start on level 1, and stay there until you've mastered it before going on to level 2. For a start that is a sure way of adding boredom to training very quickly. So don't make that mistake.

A quick example of class is:

Warming up. This should consist of simple effective joint opening exercises. This will look after our body's health, not just now but later in life. Be smart, do what complements Wing Chun.

So, let's pick a topic from level 1, say pak and punch. Work on it. Let's say half an hour. Then, introduce outside pak and cover from level 2. Work on that for a period of time. Fill a 2-hour session with the form and these two topics.

On your next session, do one of the previous and add something from level 2. Work on the things you need to. Things you feel need more work on.

You can mix and match maybe the first 2 levels for raw beginners with no experience at all. Then as they improve, start adding topics from higher levels. Try and be smart and add the things that are similar, so study the levels properly so you can judge for yourself. Make your own mix and match.

In the end, students can be given any topic from level 1 to 6 and do with ease. This is when a high level of Wing Chun is reached. Then it's just a case of keep going, it's a martial art, which means constant practice, a way of life.

LEARN IT QUICKLY,
MASTER IT IN YOUR OWN TIME.

THE LEVELS

LEVEL 1

1. Yee Gee Kim Yeung Ma.
2. Man Sau – Wu Sau.
3. Punching – Centreline.
4. Pak Sau.
5. Pak Da.
6. Jum Sau.
7. Dan Chi Sau.
8. Turning – Pivoting.
9. First Section Siu Nim Tao.

LEVEL 2

1. Punching – Elbow Out.
2. Bong Lap 1.
3. Huen Sau.
4. Outside Pak – Cover Hand.
5. Chi Sau.
6. Footwork 1.
7. Second Section Siu Nim Tao.

LEVEL 3

1. Punching - Elbow line.
2. Bong Lap 2.
3. Crossing Hands 1 – 2.
4. Inside Pak – Cover Hand.
5. Double – Single Chi Sau.
6. Footwork 2.
7. Third Section Siu Nim Tao.

LEVEL 4

1. Punching – Hooks.
2. Bong Lap 3.
3. Crossing Hands 3 – 4.
4. Cover and Follow Hands, (in and out).
5. Chi Sau (Structured and Free).
6. Footwork 3.
7. 1st Section Chum Kiu.
8. Mook Jong 1, 2, 3.

LEVEL 5

1. Punching – Body Usage, Stepping.
2. Bong Lap 4
3. Poon Sau.
4. 2 Hands on Top / Bottom.
5. Closing.
6. Gor Sau 1.
7. Footwork 4.
8. 2nd Section Chum Kiu.
9. Mook Jong 4, 5.

LEVEL 6

1. Open Hand,
2. Gor Sau 2.
3. Push / Pull.
4. Kicking.
5. Footwork 5.
6. 3rd Section Chum Kiu.
7. Mook Jong 6, 7, 8.

THE LEVELS INSIDE THE LEVELS

As you can see, inside levels 2 onwards there are specific exercises with their own levels, these are:

BONG LAP

Bong Lap 1 ----- Lap Change.
Bong Lap 2 ----- Punch Change.
Bong Lap 3 ----- Biu Change.
Bong Lap 4 ----- Gaan Change.

FOOTWORK

Footwork 1 ----- Side To Side.
Footwork 2 ----- Forward and Backwards
                 (making a square).
Footwork 3 ----- Zigzag (crossing the square).
Footwork 4 ----- Pivoting on each point of square.
Footwork 5 ----- Front leg cover, sitting on rear.

CROSSING HANDS

Crossing Hands 1 ----- Pak Da.
Crossing Hands 2 ----- Taan Da.
Crossing Hands 3 ----- Lap Da.
Crossing Hands 4 ----- Kwun Sau.

GOR SAU

Gor Sau 1 ----- Standing Still.
Gor Sau 2 ----- Moving.

An in-depth discussion and instruction on each of these exercises will follow in the LEVEL PRACTICES sections.

LEVELS PRACTICES

Practice of these levels properly will show you Wing Chun fully and correctly, while adhering to the maxims, SIMPLE, BASIC and STRAIGHTFORWARD.

A more apt saying to MY Wing Chun, which is:

LEARN IT QUICKLY,
MASTER IT IN YOUR OWN TIME.

LEVEL 1 PRACTICES

1. YEE GEE KIM YUENG MA.

Fall in and out of stance, focus on full body relaxing.

To advance this exercise, take a step forward, as your stepping foot lands bring your follow leg up level and immediately drop into Ma.

To come out of stance, place weight onto left leg and come out bringing your right leg to standing normal; next, as soon as you're normal, repeat using the right leg to step, and so on, so as both sides are getting practice.

Then, when this is done comfortably, start stepping backwards and soon it will be easy finding your OWN stance.

2. MAN SAU/WU SAU.

While standing in Y,G,K,Y,M, place your hands at the side of your chest as like the starting of forms; now, place your left hand into Taan Sau and your right hand into Wu Sau.

The Taan Sau is a short one and not an outstretched exaggerated one. Now bring back the arms to starting point. This time roll out in opposite, right hand Taan Sau and left hand Wu Sau. When this can be done easily and flowing, we can advance it.

Drop the shoulders and as the arms start to come out, open the elbow, as if stretching the lower arms from the upper arms. As in the forms, and anytime we extend the limbs, as the arms come to their stop, open the wrist joint too.

Now practise alternating with easy flow and focusing on open joints. Elbow and wrist as well as shoulders. When this can be done with ease, your structure will be at its strongest. At the same time being relaxed.

3. CENTRE LINE PUNCHING.

Using the same focus on the joints, bring your left hand knuckles to your centre with the same roll of shoulder as on the previous exercise.

Keeping the hand on centre, driving out the fist until near full extension. Joints open as it extends. Focus on raising the elbow rather just straightening the arm.

Lower the extended arm, slightly, at the same time bringing the opposite hand to centre and extending out. As the right hand is going out, bring back the left hand at the same speed, and repeat slowly to keep good form. Making sure hands go straight out and not having any circle motion which seems quite popular but a bad habit.

When this can be done comfortably and properly, then pick up the speed. Thus creating proper punching. With power.

4. PAK SAU

We have two methods of Pak Sau. A strong stopping one and a passive re-directing one.

From Man Sau/Wu Sau, bring the Wu Sau slightly out from your body so it's in line with our 2nd centre line; now with focus on the elbow, push the Pak Sau until it reaches the 2nd centre line on the other side. The arm should be bent still, not straight.

The passive Pak Sau, starting from open hands on 2nd centre line, with your right hand using a slight arc, as if you're using an elbow strike, push the elbow until the hand reaches the 3rd centre line. Your hand should be in line with your shoulder and close to your face.

Mirror practice is important as a beginner, and there is no such thing as too many drill reps.

Remember your elbow focus.

5. PAK/PUNCH

There are 2 practices for this, Pak and Punch simultaneously, the Pak Sau lands at the same time as the Punch.

And the Pak THEN Punch, as if the Pak Sau is clearing away an arm so to throw the Punch.

These are both done with the instructions on the above Punching and the Pak Sau practices.

6. JUM SAU

As a beginner and the same as everything else spoken about, do it slow.

The instructions are the same for JUM as with the above practice of Pak; the only difference is that the forearm is in contact and stays on top of the opponent's arm driving through to their centre, with the elbow focus on facing down.

7. DAN CHI SAU

There are 3 stages to our Dan Chi Sau:

1/ Strong and stopping, where we are structurally stronger than the force we are against.

2/ Passive and receiving, where we are up against a stronger force so we need to use what is Wing Chun softness.

3/ The third stage is where we take it from constant contact to starting from no contact, to actual self-defence, where it is supposed to be.

We will cover this in depth later on.

8. TURNING

See SECTION on stepping and turning for full description.

9. FIRST SECTION OF SIU NIM TAO.

See forms section.

LEVEL 2 PRACTICES

1. PUNCHING – ELBOW OUT

This punch is not just a punch, it's also a way of crushing an opponent's guard.

With your fist on centre line, slowly send it out as level 1 punch, only with this one, keep the elbow raised, pointing in the direction of where the fist is going.

The forearm looks for contact while the fist is attacking so to speak.

2. BONG LAP 1

This is a great exercise when done properly:

Player 1 holds out a right bong sau, a proper bong sau. Where the elbow is lower than the wrist.

Player 2 puts his left arm onto bong sau with elbow pointing down. Wu sau up, (important to note) a bong sau is used against an attack which is rising up, so always make sure the attacking arm is rising; any slight movement difference will make the bong not work and we move away from the bong altogether and use a different defence, which is NOT what we want at this stage. We are learning the very basic here.

Player 2 now pushes his arm and elbow forward at the same time, up slowly.
Testing.
This is teaching to use elbow energy and putting full body behind your hit.

Player 1 now using a fak sau with his left hand, makes contact with the wrist of player 2, with elbow energy on and soft shoulders, drive through, learning to feel force from contact. Now, after testing with a little force move on to learning to lap, drop the elbow while grabbing the arm of player 2 and pulling down and slightly to the left.

At the same time driving the opposite arm, in proper positions, elbow down and driving up, so player 2 can correctly use bong sau to now reverse roles.

Done slowly and with good energy you can build this drill up so you're both using really powerful arms. Which is the end result, right?

3. HUEN SAU

We all know huen sau, but just remember:

Practise standing still, turning and later stepping.

Also:

Relaxed shoulders and dropped elbow, even if the elbow has to rise a little.

Keep the intent on pointing down. For good strong force.

4. OUTSIDE PAK & COVER

This drill brings 2 moves together, the pak sau and the taan sau; though taan can and will change as the drill changes with height difference.

Use the pak sau to redirect the punch coming in.

As you pak, lift your other arm and place on the arm you're paking away; now stop, feel for pressures, test how strong you are.

The pak hand is now at wu sau positions with taan still in contact with attacking arm.

If you study yourself now, you should be in man sau/wu sau from level 1.

To make this flow, make your man sau go slightly past opponent's shoulder so his other arm, which should be up by his face, is ready to throw.

Now he throws his second hand and as it passes your man sau, pak it, and place your wu sau on his arm.

Now your on reverse side, man sau wu sau.

You can get good flow when enough practice is done.

5. CHI SAU

Here we introduce chi sau, both hands working together simultaneously.

There are a few methods to this and explained in its own section later. But introduced at level 2 here.

6. FOOTWORK 1

Footwork is simple, and when done properly, brilliant.

As I say on a regular basis, probably my most common phrase:

> WHEREVER YOU GO,
> TAKE YOUR WING CHUN WITH YOU.

Every step, movement, we do it with a straight spine, soft relaxed muscles and open joints and all movement from our centre. Then we know we move with good strong power, able to attack or defend with all we've got. Never caught out so to speak.

So, standing properly, take a step to the left, stop and feel, then take a step to the right. Only stepping to the side. One step. We are looking at keeping the same distance between our feet.

So after our step, we should be in same hip/waist/foot distance as we were in our YGKYM.

A good basic step, through practice, we will be able to stand with feet anywhere and have good structure, close or wide. Where we want our levels to take us to.

We have to start at the bottom, right?
So simple.

7. 2nd Section of Siu Nim Tao.

Follow the hints/tips in the section for form.

LEVEL 3 PRACTICES

1. PUNCHING – ELBOW IN LINE

Standing with arms up, hands on 2nd centre line.

From there, drive straightforward the fist until near full extension.

As you pull back with one arm, the other extends out in chain punch fashion.

This 3rd punch we do flows on a more natural path, so is a little easier to master.

2. BONG LAP 2

In bong lap 2 we use a punch instead of a fak and lap.

All the same as BL1 except:

Keeping elbow down, throw a punch, driving elbow up and arm forwards; on contact, stop, feel to see if you're structurally strong, if you could go through the defence if wanted, now your partner throws punch and you bong, using all the principles we look to train.

3. CROSSING HANDS 1 & 2

1/ PAK DA

2/ TAAN DA

See CROSSING HANDS SECTION for descriptions.

4. INSIDE PAK & COVER HAND.

Same as outside pak & cover only we are on the inside, more dangerous but sometimes we won't always have the best positions. So practice on the inside is good practice.

5. DOUBLE SINGLE CHI SAU.

This is where we start using a softer method, as well as two sides simultaneously working differently to the other.

Stand as in dan chi, foot on taan, now reverse with the other arms.

So all 4 arms are in contact.

Player 1 turns taan to palm and slowly tries to tap player 2 on the chin.

Player 2 uses jut sau, then with elbow down, counters with punch so as to aid in player 1 practising bong sau.

Now, just dropping the bong sau, back to starting point, repeat on other side.

With practice, a good flow can be achieved and also more force can be used to mimic strength from a real situation.

A great tool is this drill.

6. FOOTWORK 2

Following on from 1, after we step from left to right, we can now start taking it forwards and backwards.

So after taking a step to the left, take a step forward and stop.

Now, step to the right, stop.

Now step backwards.

All we are doing is stepping in a square. Simple.

7. THIRD SECTION OF SIU NIM TAO

See section on forms for descriptions...

LEVEL 4 PRACTICES

1. PUNCHING – HOOKS, ANGLES

The most important part of hooks, is to keep the shoulders open. Whether you're hooking close in or using a wider hook, shoulders open.

The 2 methods of hooking are:

A. Elbow down, vertical fist.

This is more of a either hitting through a guard or, if you're throwing a hook from where your hand already is, into an opening.

B. Elbow up, thumb down.

This is for going around a guard. Both methods when done properly have huge power behind them. If done correctly.

2. BONG LAP 3

The same principles of 1 & 2, 3 uses Biu Sau as the change. Using exactly the same energies to really work each aspects of drill.

As you shoot out the Biu and make contact, your partner goes into Bong Sau.

3. CROSSING HANDS 3 & 4

3/ LAP LAP

4/ KWUN SAU

See CROSSING HANDS SECTION for descriptions.

4. COVER AND FOLLOW HANDS

This is a great exercise to get used to sticking to arms that's coming at you random and also teaching to go on the attack from a passive position.

With hands up on 2nd centre line, your partner throws a hand to your face; as it comes in you cover it and redirect it slightly, as he brings it back to himself to throw his other hand, you keep contact with it. As he throws his other hand, do the same, now you have contact with both.

As a drill, have him keep throwing both hands while you keep contact.

After you've got used to this, you can start to learn how to follow the hand back, but instead of keeping contact, when the arm is half way back, you leave go and hit or trap or push. We call this sneaking in under cover.

Remember and do both sides.

You'll find you can hit, control or just go to Man Sau Wu Sau. Remember proper form at all times.

5. CHI SAU – STRUCTURED

This structured Chi Sau is more for building up our soft/relaxed body structure, so we can learn to be as strong as possible while being as soft as possible.

See CHI SAU SECTION for descriptions.

6. FOOTWORK 3

So far we are making a square, now we are going to cross the square. PICTURE YOUR SQUARE in your head, or even draw it out on the floor.

Standing properly, after going left, then forwards, then right and backwards; now instead of going left again, take a step to the top left corner, now sideways to the right.

Now instead of going straight back, go to left bottom.

So what we are doing now is learning to move sideways and forwards/backwards. Very simple, like it is supposed to be, right?

7. FIRST SECTION CHUM KIU

Yes, Chum Kiu already, remember this saying:

> LEARN IT QUICKLY,
> MASTER IT IN YOUR OWN TIME.

See FORMS SECTION for descriptions.

8. MOOK JONG. 1,2,3

The wooden dummy is a great tool and forms differ from school to school. So practice on the dummy is your personal training.

I introduce it here, quite early compared to some schools, as it will work alongside our footwork and Chum Kiu.

In my view they both complement each other.

None of this, oh I can't do dummy until I learn final form. Or, only special students get shown it. That's nonsense,

It's only held back for financial gain in my opinion.

LEVEL 5 PRACTICES

1. PUNCHING – BODY USAGE

Now we are stepping, hitting with proper body alignment, or at least getting there, we can now add the hits to our movements, it will add our body mass to our hitting structure. Even more power, and making us better equipped to handle ourselves.

So all the punching we add with every step. So lots to practise still.

Add a hit to every step, as foot lands, hand lands.

Building up to throwing combinations when you get more experience. SHADOW FIGHTING.

2. BONG LAP 4

Here we will use a low hit so Gaan Sau can be used to drill.

Using alongside Bong Lap 1, 2 and 3, every now and then throw a low hook,

Gaan Sau stops, then the hitter changes his direction of force to raise up so the Gaan Sau turns to bong sau. To keep flowing.

When experience has been gained you can add it all together changing at random to gain more confidence.

3. POON SAU/ CONTROLLING

This is where we can close our arms in while keeping our elbow energy on.

Control of centre. So we can be out quite wide and in very tight with the same strong feeling and safety.

4. TWO HANDS ON TOP / BOTTOM.

Here we get to go over techniques if we find ourselves either with our hands both on top of opponent or underneath.

From just rolling, close or wide we find the paths to either hitting or trapping.

There aren't any set moves as such, just find what comes at that specific time.

5. CLOSING / CONTROLLING.

In this section we use stand-up grappling and controlling for when distance has been dictated by opponent or we are caught unaware.

Class is needed for this training, as putting it on paper is very hard.

6. GOR SAU 1

The introduction of free fighting/self-defence when done properly can be taught very easily and to a very high standard, to even the most timid.

We will look into this in closer details at a different time.

7. FOOTWORK 4

OK, we can now go forwards, backwards, side-to-side and angles forward and backwards. Level 4 is going to teach us to pivot/turn on each step.

After taking a step, any step, turn on left foot to change angle of attack.

Now your square has changed direction, so turn back on other foot to end up back at the start. This way both sides get drilled.

Now this has added a whole new level of footwork for us. We can move anywhere.

8. 2ND SECTION OF CHUM KIU

See FORMS SECTION for descriptions.

9. MOOK JONG 4 & 5

The next 2 sections of the dummy.

LEVEL 6 PRACTICES

1. OPEN HAND STRIKING

As the header says, open hand. So incorporate all the hitting spoken about, only now we use open hands, fingers, palms, knife edge and grabbing.

Probably the most lethal.

Hand conditioning is a must for this which is incorporated into a student's schedule before reaching this level.

2. GOR SAU 2

We go up to top level here where a student will be comfortable and confident and very good at free fighting and defence scenarios. As it's built up gradually to high level.

3 PUSH/PULL

Here we use the grabbing of arms, clothing, to build up our structural power to control a situation without the need for striking. It's not always about punching.

Body angles and energies worked on.

4. KICKING

The introduction of kicks, to add to our ability.

Wing Chun kicking is devastating, attacking the lower half. The same methods of open shoulders apply to the hips/waist.

See KICKING SECTION for descriptions.

5. FOOTWORK 5

The last footwork drill. Adding the most common of stances, the one foot in front of the other, to protect our lower half, groin.

Standing in Biu Ma, step the square, keeping in Biu Ma. Simple.

That's it for FOOTWORK. Stepping in a square and crossing it, how easy and straightforward. No need for fancy patterns. SIMPLE.

6. 3RD SECTION CHUM KIU.

See FORMS SECTION for descriptions

7. MOOK JONG 6, 7, 8.

The final 3 sections of dummy.

PRACTICES
THE PUNCHING

Wing Chun is a striking art, whether it be fists, palms or fingers or the feet. We practise hitting. To me it's the bread and butter of the art.

Yes we have all the techniques for stopping or redirecting, but it's the short-range striking with power, together with the rapid-fire punching that has given it a good reputation for street defence. Overwhelming hitting if you like.

Pretty much from week one of training, our classes and self-practice at home consists of chain punching. We've all been there, seeing how many punches we can throw in a minute.

So let's do it properly.

HINTS/TIPS/DRILLS

Very important to remember from the start, the arm must never be fully extended, very dangerous for the elbow. Always keep it 'just inside' fully extended.

As the arm extends, focus on opening the shoulders, then elbows and then near the end the wrists open. And when bringing back the arms to starting point they close.

Takes practice but that's the importance of how we gain power. To bring on a student properly. For maximum power. Always relaxed arms.

When throwing hands, I always use a phrase I think is important:

ALWAYS MAKE THE SECOND HAND AVAILABLE.

In other words, keep them up, always plan your second hit as your first one is en route. And by second hand I mean, 3rd 4th 5th etc., etc.

Don't rely on one hit working.

AND, always use focus intention. Wherever you're planning on hitting, have that forward, focused intention.

IT'S HEADING THERE, SO IT'S GOING THERE. Attitude if you like.

REMEMBER, focus on bottom 3 knuckles hitting contact.

Raising of elbow and not just putting the fist out. This method makes defending it much more difficult as well as adding power and speed.

Soft knuckles, not clenched. My thumb tip is touching middle joint of first finger. Whether a straight punch or hook, bottom 3 knuckles are the contact.

Use that same focus on going forwards as using those knuckles for contact too.

Quick one on breathing: lots of people exhale on execution of hit, nothing wrong with that way at all, it's tried and tested. What I practise, is what we can call freestyle breathing – doesn't matter whether my hands are hitting or defending or just held up in front.

NATURAL BREATH.

Just breathe normally, in and out. Practise throwing chain punching while just breathing. You'll keep your energy longer.

PUNCHING DRILLS

We work up from 1 to 5 at class, depending on experience. If it's your first day, just do number 1, until you get it done properly. Then moving on to the next stage. But as with everything, even when we are great at it, mastered it, we still do it. We leave nothing behind here as it's all important to do for as long as we continue training.

EACH LEVEL PUNCHING IS ADDED TO EACH OF THESE EXERCISES.

1. STANDING STILL. Feet flat on floor, just concentrating on the hitting.

2. HEEL BOUNCE. Standing on toes, as the arm reaches its imaginary target, the heels hit the floor. Working up to left hand hitting, left heel down; right hand hitting, right heel down. A good exercise for hand-feet coordinating.

3. FORWARD/BACKWARDS stepping. Using the toes in line with arch footwork, step forward, as foot lands, hand lands. Alternate left foot right hand / right foot left hand, what I call CROSS BODY HITTING.

To same side hitting, left foot lands, left hand lands. Easier to get caught off balance but we must train for such scenarios.

4. SIDEWAYS. Same as above only going side to side. Remember to cross body hit and same side hit.

5. SQUARE HITTING. Using the 5 punches from the levels and adding to our 5 levels of footwork.

That's a class progression of punch drilling.

THE 5 PUNCHES

1. CENTRE LINE PUNCHING
2. ELBOW OUT PUNCHING
3. ELBOW LINE PUNCHING
4. HOOKING PUNCHING

5. UPPER CUTS

Yes, hooks and upper cuts. Who said Wing Chun was only straight hitting.

ABSOLUTELY NOT.

REMEMBER THE STEPPING RULE, see the STEPPING section.

PRACTICES

KICKING

Wing Chun kicks are short, low and very powerful, if we adhere to the same principles as the arms, where we loosen and open the shoulders, well for kicking we loosen and open the hips and waist. Then the knee and ankle. The moment we lift the knee, the hip joint opens, drops down. As the leg goes to target, the knee and ankle open. Whether we are kicking straight or doing a rounding kick, it's done this way. Upper body stays straight, the power from the centre as with the arms. If done properly, the power that can be generated is immense. So, don't neglect the legs, they will come in handy sometime.

There is a saying I often see:

Fear not the man who practises 100s of kicks 100s of times. Fear the man who practises 1 kick 10,000 times.

Often neglected, kicking is a crucial part of Wing Chun, So get kicking in your daily practice. Kicking a bag is what we NEED, the only thing that will bring on power as well as conditioning.

A full and detailed section will be available at a later date.

PRACTICES
STEPPING/TURNING

I use a saying most class times:

> WHEREVER YOU GO,
> TAKE YOUR WING CHUN WITH YOU.

It means stepping, moving properly so we don't put ourselves in a weak position.

The square stepping in each of the levels is so easy and simple. Which is what we want.

Always remember to add these hints, tips into it to maximise your training.

Move as one unit, don't let your bottom half move separate to your top half.

To train this, stand in Biu Ma, one foot in front of the other, on a tightrope as we say, with a partner placing his hand on your knee, try stepping and moving him – with practice he will be able to add more pressure each time and you'll be able to move him. Then, when this is done with ease, change your stance to toes to arch and parallel. So we practise each of our methods.

Remember to move with your centre.

And straight spine. ALWAYS. And the hip joints open, just like the shoulders.

Going forward, backwards or sideways – always have that one unit movement.

Imagine having a heavy object on the floor, and you want to move it, not kick it with your foot, using your body. You'll soon get it. And be good at it. It will add so much soft power to your structure.

When turning, Pivoting, turn on your heels, and when possible, turn one at a time. Keeping 3 points of the feet in touch with floor at all times. Mentally use that same focus as stepping, as if moving a heavy weight with your knee.

3 places for our feet, our stances:

Standing in YGKYM, parallel
Toes in line with arch
One foot in front of the other

Practise these in the square stepping and any other drill where we move, step. Turn.

You'll find, with practice, that you will be able to have your feet quite close together and still have immense power because we go from using the ground to using our spine. Remember, we are training to master it.

THE 5 LEVELS OF STEPPING

1   side to side
2   forwards and backwards
3   crossing the square
4   pivot, turn on each point of square
5   front leg cover, sitting on rear leg

Lots of coaches, Sifu, teachers, don't show footwork because that's what they rely on when they come up against someone with same or better level of hands.

They move. The best defence ever, is to not be there.

HAPPY STEPPING...

PRACTICES
CROSSING HANDS

The crossing hands drills are really good for building up close-up, in-your-face confidence, as it's the first two hand exercises where two hands are working for both partners at the same time. Set moves inside chi sau is all it is, but teaches loads. It gives an idea, under controlled manner, of loose hands coming at you and it is also good for building up reaction speed. Done right will develop great skill.

Firstly, we have to make sure we have contact on the right parts of the arm. We DO NOT go wrist-to-wrist in any way, whether it's this drill or chi sau or self-defence scenarios. We see lots rolling wrist-to-wrist, they have their reasons obviously, but we DON'T.

Whenever we have contact we use the strongest part of the forearms, 2 to 3 inches up from wrist. Not only is it strong, it makes it easy to go through other techniques. If we have contact on the correct part, any movement closer to the wrist or to the elbow makes transition to another technique easy. But the fundamental reason, it's stronger.

The weakest part of the arm, is the wrist. As I learnt a long time ago, to control the arm, go for the wrist.

To control the body, go for the elbow.

So we stay away from them on ourselves. We attack them with the strong part.

So ALWAYS use the right part.

CROSSING HANDS 1   PAK DA

From rolling, player 1 pulls down on player 2 bong sau, as he does this, player 2 learns to react by throwing a punch with his other hand.

As the punch comes in, player 1 uses pak sau and punch to counter, then as player 2 learns not to freeze by throwing his other hand, player 1 now using the same pak and punch for that.

This drill, when done with practice, can be a very useful drill for both players regardless of what role they are playing.

CROSSING HANDS 2   TAN DA

Same rules as 1, only this time, using a taan instead of pak. This is to be done standing still, turning and stepping. Depending on your level.

CROSSING HANDS 3   LAP DA

As above, only using a lap sau and punch instead of pak or taan.

CROSSING HANDS 4   KWUN SAU

Again, as above only using kwun sau.

Stepping and or turning is to be added to each drill as staying put can get you in trouble. Anyway, safer to move than depend on a technique. If it doesn't work then at least you're not there taking one.

One of my favourite exercises is CROSSING HANDS, we get a lot from it when we know what we are looking for.

PRACTICES
THE FORMS

The first 2 forms of Wing Chun are so underrated by so many, myself included in the beginning. Only after many years and much practice, and missed practice I must add, that I came to realise their importance. When I was told forms must be done daily, I thought it was just a rumour. Only now figuring out it wasn't just words.

I'm not going to write down how to do the form, I think that's impossible, but what I will do is stress some important points as I would in class. You can learn the form at a class of your choice, it will no doubt vary from school to school but some points are important to whichever one it is.

When the arms are extended, open joints, from shoulder to fingers. Regardless of what techniques you're using.

Softly raise the head and turn the hips, go for a straight spine.

Breathe in the belly, as low as possible.

Relax and focus on just your skeletal moving.

Use intent for every move. Going out or coming back.

Do it slow. It really does take time to incorporate everything.

Learning the turns and axis in Chum Kiu needs class time. Get it in.

What some perceive to be defence moves in the form are what I train as attacking moves. Not everything is what some teach to be right. Or what it may look like.

Another important factor when doing first form, it teaches us forward intention, meaning we always look to attack, even if we are stepping to the side or even backwards, our intent is still going forwards, it adds power to our arms, hands or legs, whatever the weapon is we are using at that moment.

So just standing in YGKYM is a lesson in itself.

So to learn the forms, get to class. Get the hours in. They really do have so much inside them. Not just external but mentally too, gives us grounding and calmness.

BRINGING THE LEVELS ALIVE

After all, we are all doing training for one thing – to look after ourselves and family if the need arises. We are not doing it so we don't have to fight, as they say in films.

So, while doing forms, drills, solo practice, set training with a partner and everything else we do is all good, there must be a stage where we put it all to practise against reality, or as damn close as possible. Pressure-tested if you like. But done properly.

How many video clips do we see of one guy throwing a punch, his partner then doing his thing and you know it's not going to be like that for real. Some we see that's laughable. It has to be done honestly or it won't work and we'll get hurt.

Firstly, let's have a quick few words on aggression, we need it. Period. It's not as simple as, just losing the rag, going in wild. It needs to be controlled, so you don't go too far, by too far I mean where you're needing to be pulled off someone. You may end up on the wrong side of the law. We need to be sensible at the same time as going nuts.

Aggression needs to be switched on and off like a light switch. Hard to do but it's achievable with the right training. That is the type we want and need. Maybe that's the way of martial arts, to be nice until it's time to not be nice. Going mental but under our control. Typed with a smile.

At class time I do specific things that can help build aggression – I call it bottle building, very effective and quickly learned. We will be covering this topic at another time in the future.

When it's a fight or a self-defence situation, aggression is needed. Lots fail not because of their ability, but their own fear, in their head. Lost even before anything happens. At the talking stage even.

With it though we need the right training so that we are capable. So, alongside BOTTLE BUILDING, we bring our levels alive, doing specific training which allows a student to improve his ability, regardless of what level he is at. Regardless of his personality, whether he's a born killer or a Mr 'soft as sponge'. Whether he's on his first week or month or his second year or longer. We practise.

A little glimpse of a session could be:

Taking a topic from any level,

and…

SOME ALIVE TRAINING…

Take each move from every level, standing toe-to-toe and static. Player 1 tries to touch with fingertips, player 2 practises his technique. Take your time. Get it right. Build up the speed as ability improves.

When it comes to stepping, only use one step per move/technique. We need to get really good, confident before moving on, this way will make a good fighter out of anyone. Building up properly step by step will get us there. No ego remember.

Full random Movement is introduced in GOR SAU. GOR SAU is introduced when the above is done to a good standard.

Remember, it's not going to be pretty.

PRETTY KUNG FU ISN'T GOOD, GOOD KUNG FU ISN'T PRETTY.

GOR SAU 1 & 2

Start off toe-to toe.

Player 1 tries touching, slowly, with fingertips.

Player 2 uses a technique from a level he is on.

Starting off just standing still.

Go from just using left hand or right hand and use random. Go from standing still, going through all the stepping levels.

Where you build up to random stepping.

1/ only use left hand
2/ only use right hand
3/ only use straight hits
4/ only use hooks
5/ random.

Add different techniques each time until you're doing the ones you know to a very good standard.

In time this method gets you both working freely and with twitch-like speed, to such an extent that you'll both be using some good intent in both attacking and defending, as you become familiar with your partner and his ability to stay safe.

The 6 levels, let's be honest, are very much nothing, easily learned over a short space of time. So, alive training will be pretty much most of class time for those who master the levels, so fighting should be as easy as after a certain period.

So, doing it this way, will build up your confidence in self-defence and fighting.

Or you can walk away. Smiles.

INTERNAL OR EXTERNAL

My personal view.

As far back as I can remember, and also read, it's always been WING CHUN. So when was the introduction of 'internal wing chun' or 'external wing chun'? As if two different styles.

Have I missed something? As it seems only lately that it's been flung about. Is it that it's only just been discovered as being trained at the beginning or, is it because other systems are mixed with it over recent times through certain Sifu not fully learning Wing Chun and then searching other styles for the internal?

Whatever reasons, my beliefs are that all styles, systems, strive for that INTERNAL relaxed softness. There is no need to add another style to Wing Chun to achieve any internal. I believe this art has it all, if given the time and proper instruction.

So what is Wing Chun really?

For long enough there has been a war of words between many, both SIFU and students alike, on the subject of internal and external.

Which is it?

Well, for me, Wing Chun softness isn't tai chi softness. Or any other internal art that goes the same as tai chi. As I stated earlier, no need for other styles.

For me, Wing Chun softness is this:

If my arm meets yours, and I can feel I'm stronger, by having good structure and not muscle strength, then I'm going to go through your arm and hit. My focus and intention is on. I will strike.

If I feel that my opponent is stronger, then, because of my training, the sensitivity training from chi sau, I will feel this and change direction, either by just changing the angle of my arm, the drop or raise of elbow as a simple example, or adjusting my body a little different. Or by using footwork to go a different way. If I have to change, I will.

I certainly won't become soft in the arms when there isn't a need and likewise neither will I try and force through when I know it's a struggle. I will keep my focus and energy going forward. It's all down to our training to tell us which way we go. To me, that's the meaning of sensitivity training from dan chi or chi sau or poon sau. That is Wing Chun, not internal or external, just WING CHUN.

Use this saying for keeping yourselves right…

FIND THE QUICKEST WAY, WITH THE LEAST RESISTANCE.

So I train to be as strong as possible, but not muscle strong, skeletal strong. Structure strong. Soft and relaxed muscles while being as strong as, is for me what Wing Chun was before the introduction of other arts into it. People watering it down.

My WING CHUN always trains to be structure strong as I call it, proper alignment of the body.

All 6 points. WRIST, ELBOW, SHOULDER, HIP, KNEE, ANKLE, in alignment.

That's not to say I'm not relaxed, we have to be relaxed at all times. Being relaxed as possible during training so we can take it into a situation is what I think is the aim of any art, the holy grail if you like.

There is no need to go all floppy or rolling hands so they end up at waist height. Pointless rolling is what I'd call that. You can use another of my usual class sayings, and probably most fighting arts classes, HANDS UP AT ALL TIMES.

So if your hands are up, and Wing Chun says the quickest route from A to B is a straight line, then your hands are going from up near your face to the nearest target, most likely his face. Closest weapon to nearest target. Hands down at your waist is for an emergency block, nothing else.

The only training I do where the arms are silly soft is when I'm teaching students to let their arms go if or when they are grabbed and trying to be pulled. Teaching them to just give the arm and not the body. That is the only reason I do soft arms.

So let's train Wing Chun.

As the heading at the top states, it's my view, my opinion. We're all entitled as they say. I'm using my entitlement.

CONCLUSION

When you think about it, it's nothing really. My levels, or system if you prefer. What I've tried to do throughout this last 10 years of training, is cut out the unnecessary pointless rubbish and only do what works. Making it simple. I have spent countless hours doing certain drills, techniques, trying to get them perfect. Only to realise this far down the line, it was a waste of time. Not all of it obviously, but far too much of it.

Or, maybe, the pointless stuff WAS part of training, to help me realise its non-effectiveness to get to this point in time. A case of, seeing the rubbish to be able to recognise what is good.

Either way, I'm here now, at this point, doing what I believe to be a great art, practising only what is needed.

Fighting is straightforward and ugly. Am I wrong in saying that training should be the same, to replicate as close as possible to real fight time. It's my opinion, that back at the very beginning, Wing Chun was more like what I'm doing now.

I'm not saying I've found the true, original Wing Chun, far from it, but I do believe it's been buttered up so much that it's lost its cause. Got lost among the flowery stuff which seems to be more popular these days. Watered down, unrecognisable in some cases.

Again, I'll emphasise, we are all different and have our own views, this book and contents are mine.

So if you're training Wing Chun and you're doing your drills, ask yourself – is it going to work or are you just going to look good? And when I say look good, I mean for that split second, because if it's just looking good and not practical then you're not going to look good for very long. Always take a step out of yourself, and honestly look at what you're doing and question everything, Ask if you're unsure. Ask yourself, when in practice:

Does it look like nothing, but works? YES.

Does it look really easy and straightforward? YES.

Does it work in full-on scenario training with no compliant partners? YES.

Then to me, it's pretty much Wing Chun, it's meant to look like nothing. But boy it's good when it's done right.

HAPPY TRAINING.

www.ingramcontent.com/pod-product-compliance
Ingram Content Group UK Ltd.
Pitfield, Milton Keynes, MK11 3LW, UK
UKHW042000230426
12048UKWH00009B/450